Author:
David Stewart has written many nonfiction books for children. He lives in Brighton, England, with his family.

Artist:
David Antram was born in Brighton, England, in 1958. He studied at Eastbourne College of Art and then worked in advertising for 15 years before becoming a full-time artist. He has illustrated many children's nonfiction books.

Series creator:
David Salariya was born in Dundee, Scotland. He has illustrated a wide range of books and has created and designed many new series for publishers in the UK and overseas. David established The Salariya Book Company in 1989. He lives in Brighton with his wife, illustrator Shirley Willis, and their son, Jonathan.

Editor: **Nick Pierce**

Photo credits:
p.22–23 Alex Cimbal/Shutterstock, Milan Boers/Wikimedia Commons, mliu92/Wikimedia Commons, Ami Parikh/Shutterstock, Tory Kallman/Shutterstock
p.24–25 Tory Kallman/Shutterstock, Four Oaks/Shutterstock, Elise V/Shutterstock, Shane Gross/Shutterstock, COULANGES/Shutterstock, Dotted Yeti/Shutterstock

Published in Great Britain in MMXXI by
Book House, an imprint of
The Salariya Book Company Ltd
25 Marlborough Place, Brighton BN1 1UB
www.salariya.com

ISBN: 978-1-913337-74-2

SCRIBO   BOOK HOUSE   SCRIBBLERS

© The Salariya Book Company Ltd MMXXI

1 3 5 7 9 8 6 4 2

A CIP catalogue record for this book is available from the British Library.
Printed and bound in China.

Visit
www.salariya.com
for our online catalogue and
free fun stuff.

PAPER FROM
SUSTAINABLE
FORESTS

E-book version available.

How Would You Survive as a Killer Whale?

Written by
David Stewart

Illustrated by
David Antram

Series created by
David Salariya

BOOK HOUSE
a SALARIYA imprint

Contents

You are a killer whale

You might be called a killer whale, but you're actually the largest species of dolphin. You are also known as an orca. All dolphins belong to a big group of animals called toothed whales. You are a very social animal, living together with other killer whales in family groups that exhibit very complex, learned behaviours. Even though you're the top of the food chain in the oceans where you live, being a killer whale can be difficult and challenging: you have to hunt for food, raise your young and keep track of your family. You're also at risk from human-made pollution, which can affect your food supply. It's time to answer the big question: how would you survive as a killer whale?

A killer whale's body

Melon

This rounded part of your forehead is what you use for echolocation. You make high-pitched sounds that pass through the melon, which focuses the sounds and projects them into the water. The sounds bounce off nearby objects and return to you as an echo, giving you the locations of the objects.

Dorsal fin

This large fin on your back helps keep you balanced as you swim. An adult male's dorsal fin can be up to 1.8 metres (6 feet) tall.

Teeth

You have 40 very sharp, interlocking teeth. *Chomp!*

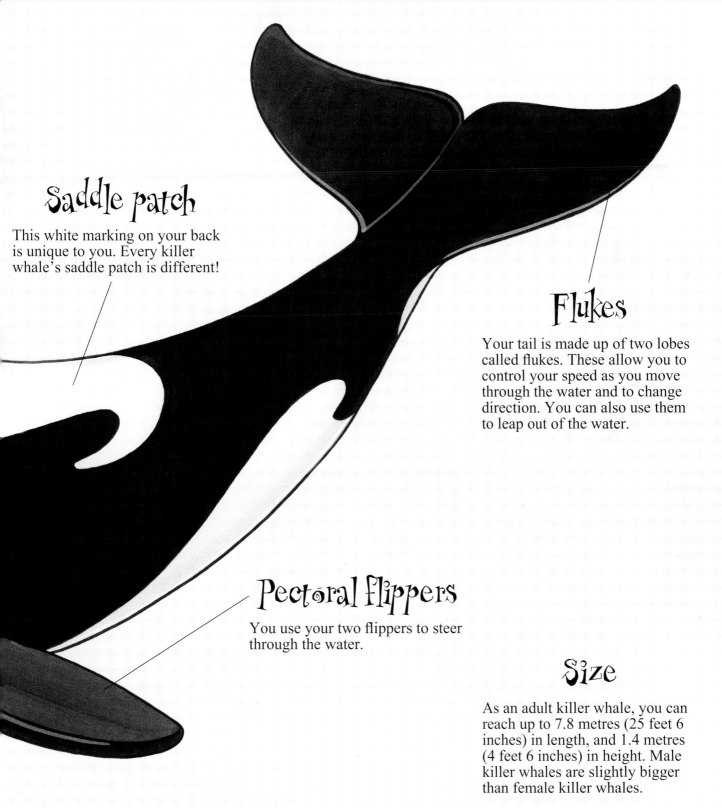

Saddle patch

This white marking on your back is unique to you. Every killer whale's saddle patch is different!

Flukes

Your tail is made up of two lobes called flukes. These allow you to control your speed as you move through the water and to change direction. You can also use them to leap out of the water.

Pectoral flippers

You use your two flippers to steer through the water.

Size

As an adult killer whale, you can reach up to 7.8 metres (25 feet 6 inches) in length, and 1.4 metres (4 feet 6 inches) in height. Male killer whales are slightly bigger than female killer whales.

Saving your breath

You might spend most of your time living, socialising, travelling and hunting under the water, but killer whales are actually air-breathing animals, like all mammals. This means that you need to rise to the surface regularly in order to take new air into your lungs. You breathe through the blowhole at the top of your head. Once you sink back down below the surface again, your blowhole closes with a watertight seal to prevent you from drowning. This means that the whole time you're underwater, you're actually holding your breath!

If you...

are a newborn killer whale, you will be born underwater, and the first thing you need to do is to swim to the surface to fill your lungs with air. As you swim up, make sure to keep your blowhole closed!

I'd better breathe again – it's been almost 15 minutes!

Adult killer whales usually stay underwater for about 2.3 minutes. But on deep dives, down to as much as 100 metres (328 feet) below the surface, you can hold your breath for as long as 15 minutes.

100 metres (328 feet)

Killer whales are called 'voluntary breathers'. This means that, unlike most animals, which breathe automatically, you have to decide when you want to breathe.

You breathe out stale air through your blowhole, making a spout of water droplets called a blow. Then you breathe in to refill your lungs with air.

You can't breathe through your mouth and don't have a nose. Instead, your blowhole is like your nostrils.

Did you see a penguin swimming quickly through the water? That would make a tasty snack. Quick, beat your tail harder to move faster and catch it!

Built for speed

You are the fastest toothed whale in the ocean. Your normal 'cruising' speed is about 10 kilometres per hour (6.2 miles per hour), but you can reach a top speed of around 50 kph (31 mph). This is faster than the speed limit for a car that is travelling in a residential area. Your body has a smooth, streamlined shape, perfect for swimming at fast speeds through water without encountering much resistance. You move your large, powerful tail up and down to go forward.

If you...

are feeling social, why not leap out of the water to display it to the rest of your family? This is called breaching.

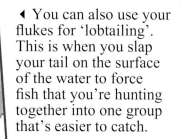

◀ You can also use your flukes for 'lobtailing'. This is when you slap your tail on the surface of the water to force fish that you're hunting together into one group that's easier to catch.

▶ You might also feel like lying on your side and splashing the water surface with your pectoral fins. It's thought that you might do this fin slap to send signals to others.

▲ If you want to increase your speed, you can 'porpoise'. This is when you breach the surface and dive over and over again as you move forward.

11

There are some walruses dozing
on a beach near the water's edge.
Quick, launch a surprise attack
and you can eat one for dinner.
It'll be a change from fish!

A very unfussy eater

As an apex predator, you sit at the top of the ocean's food chain and can enjoy eating all kinds of delicious prey. You need to consume about 250 kilograms (551 pounds) of food every day to survive as an adult orca. Although much of your menu is to be found in the water, you can also feast on animals of the land and air – whether by grabbing seabirds that have settled on the surface of the water, or seizing unsuspecting seals or walruses off beaches.

Your diet might include:

1. Grey whale calf
2. Fish
3. Seal
4. Dolphin
5. Manatee
6. Squid
7. Penguin
8. Sea turtle

If you...

would like a change in cuisine, why not try to catch a moose or caribou? Orcas attack these land animals as they swim across sea channels, moving from one feeding ground to another.

Different families of killer whales have different diets. Each family passes down the hunting techniques for catching its favourite prey to new generations.

Wolves of the sea

Killer whales are sometimes called the 'wolves of the sea', because you hunt your prey in packs, just like wolves do on land. You use echolocation to find your prey: you make clicking sounds and listen for echoes as the clicks bounce off other nearby animals. You can tell what kind of prey it is from the different echoes. Say you've found a grey whale calf. Now all the whales in your group need to swim together around it, herding it into a small circle where it will be easier to attack and kill. You use your sharp teeth to rip and tear at your prey, and because your teeth point backward, it is difficult for your prey to escape their grip.

If you...

are feeling bored, you can play with your food. A killer whale might 'play' with a sea lion, using its mighty tail like a bat to bounce the sea lion's body high into the air.

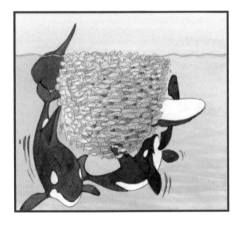

▲ To hunt a school of fish, you circle around them, spinning your bodies, blowing bubbles and making loud bursts of sound to herd them together so that they're easier to eat.

▲ When hunting a great white shark, you harass the animal until it is exhausted and then body slam it to flip it onto its back. Now it is stunned and unable to move, and much easier to finish off.

▼ You can use teamwork to nab a seal sitting on an ice floe. All of the whales in your group line up and charge at the seal, using your flukes to push the water and create a rolling wave that knocks the seal off and into your jaws.

You'll work together as a team to hunt and eat this grey whale calf. It doesn't stand a chance against your herding technique, speed and sharp teeth!

You've come across another pod
with a dialect that's similar to
your own. They must be your
relatives. Now your two pods
can swim along together for a
while, using your shared dialect to
communicate.

Family life

Like all killer whales, you will spend your entire life living with your family group, which is called a pod. All of the whales in a pod are related on the mother's side of the family. Pods can range in size enormously, from only four whales to more than fifty! Each pod has its own dialect – a unique combination of calls and whistles – passed down from one generation to the next. You use these sounds to communicate with the other whales in your pod. Closely related pods may use these sounds to identify one another when swimming in the same area so that they can get together to socialise.

If you...

want to comfort another member of your pod, rub up against them. This is how killer whales frequently show support and affection to each other.

Killer whale pods are matriarchal, which means that the oldest female is in charge.

Children, parents, grandparents and even great-grandparents can all live together in a pod!

Pods sometimes break up for a few hours into groups travelling in the same direction but up to 6.4 kilometres (4 miles) apart. The mature males will travel in one group, and the females and immature males in another.

17

Raising a calf

As a female killer whale, you won't typically start to mate until you're about 15 years old. Killer whales can choose to mate at any time of the year, but tend to favour periods when there is lots of food around to eat. Once you're pregnant, it'll be 17 to 18 months before you're ready to give birth to your calf. Once the calf has emerged, usually tail-first, you will help it to the surface to take its first breath. Your calf will stay close by your side for the next two years, then it will start to move away and hunt with the rest of the pod.

If you...

are a killer whale born in captivity, your lifespan will be shorter than that of your wild relatives. In the wild, a female can live as long as 80 to 90 years, but a male can live only up to 50 years.

◀ It takes three to five years for a female killer whale to become pregnant again after having a calf. And female killer whales stop breeding at the age of 40. This means that you're only likely to have four to six calves in your lifetime.

▲ Female orcas do not usually mate with close male relatives. When meeting another pod, you listen for a male making whistling sounds that are distinct from those of your own family's dialect.

(1) Female orcas usually only give birth to one calf at a time. Only one instance of a killer whale giving birth to twins has been recorded. (2) You feed your calf with milk, which you squirt into its mouth. Your milk is 30 to 50 percent fat, which helps build up your calf's blubber. This will keep them insulated in the water.

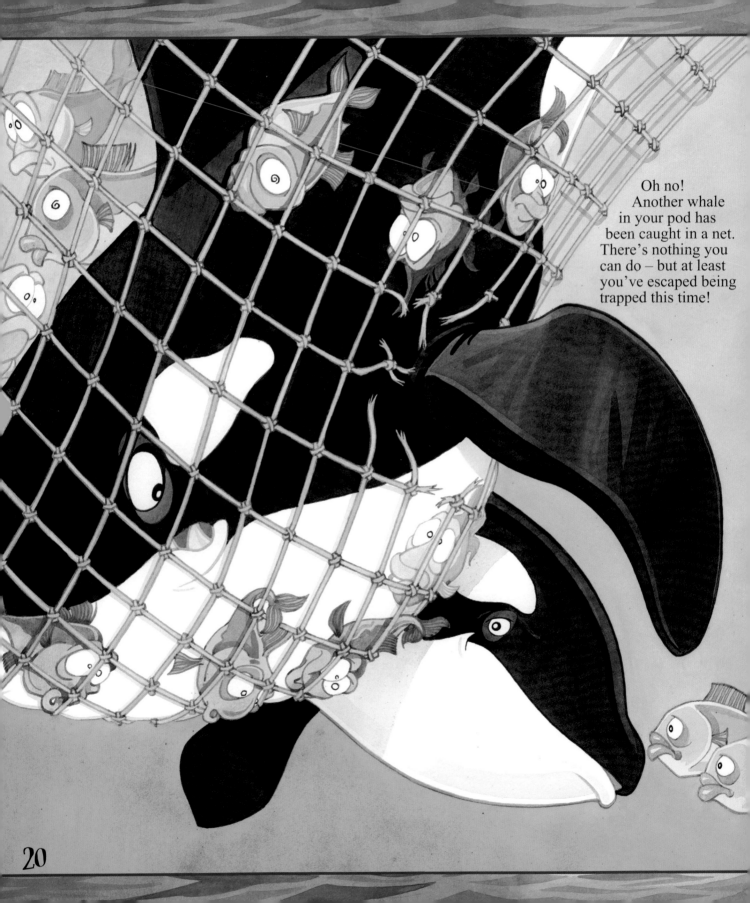

Oh no!
Another whale
in your pod has
been caught in a net.
There's nothing you
can do – but at least
you've escaped being
trapped this time!

What are the dangers?

Even though killer whales have never been hunted in large numbers, industrial-scale fishing means that killer whales like you sometimes get trapped in nets meant for catching other species. The food you eat can also contain invisible hazards, like poisonous substances that will damage your health. And there's also the possibility that you'll be captured and sold as a tourist attraction to a sea life park, which can negatively affect your mental health and well-being, especially if you are separated from your pod.

If you...

have a dorsal fin that is bent over, you're probably stressed and unhappy. Your dorsal fin should be upright. This often happens to killer whales in captivity.

Fishermen have been known to use guns and explosives to kill orca pods that they've blamed for eating too many fish.

Toxins dumped into the sea can work their way up the food chain from plankton that have absorbed them, to the kind of prey eaten by killer whales. Because you're an apex predator, you can end up consuming very concentrated doses of these toxins.

Most killer whales in captivity have been taken from the wild. Very few are born in zoos or sea life parks.

The Story Of Tilikum

Covered in detail in the award-winning 2013 documentary film *Blackfish*, the story of Tilikum the killer whale is quite a controversial one. Tilikum eventually became a popular tourist attraction at SeaWorld in Orlando, Florida, where he performed shows. However, he was involved in the deaths of three people, including one of his trainers. The documentary alleges that his story exposes the way that killer whales can suffer in captivity, affecting their behaviour.

1. Tilikum was captured off the coast of Iceland in 1983 when he was two years old, and was separated from his wild family.

2. *As an adult orca, Tilikum was 6.7 metres (22 feet) long and weighed 5,443 kilograms (12,000 pounds).*

3. *His former trainers and the makers of Blackfish claim that the stresses of his new life as a captive whale led to his killing three people. It is alleged that killer whales at these tourist attractions are often bullied by the other whales they're kept with, and subjected to busy performance schedules, causing them distress.*

4. *Tilikum died in captivity at the age of 36 in 2017, after a long illness. Tilikum's story has changed public attitudes toward killer whale captivity and shows. SeaWorld announced that they would stop making orcas perform at their parks.*

5. *Many scientific experts and animal rights activists have called on these wildlife amusement parks to release their animals back into the wild or into animal sanctuaries where they can lead lives closer to their natural habitat.*

Killer whale family tree

Killer whales, also known as orcas, are a species of toothed whale, or odontocetes. Toothed whales include dolphins, porpoises and whales with teeth. Killer whales, despite their name, are actually a type of oceanic dolphin. All toothed whales are related and share the same ancient common ancestor that lived many millions of years ago. If you were a killer whale, these would be some of your closest cousins...

Orca (You)

These large, highly intelligent and social dolphins are identifiable by their distinctive white and black markings.

Bottlenose Dolphin

These silvery-grey dolphins are found in warm waters around the world. They communicate with one another using a complex system of squeaks and whistle sounds.

Porpoise

The smallest species of toothed whale. Porpoises, although closely related to dolphins, tend to have smaller mouths, different from the elongated beaks of dolphin species.

Sperm Whale

This is the largest of the species of toothed whale. They have enormous heads, with very large, rounded foreheads.

Amazon River Dolphin

These are a species of freshwater dolphin. The adults have a pink colour to their skin. They are the largest species of river dolphin.

Narwhal

This species' famous tusk is actually an overgrown, protruding tooth. They live in the Arctic waters of Norway, Russia, Canada and Greenland.

Killer whale quiz

1 What is the name of the unique marking on a killer whale's back?

2 What does a killer whale breathe through?

3 What is a killer whale's top speed?

4 How many pounds of food do you need to eat every day to survive as an adult orca?

5 What is the name for the system of clicks and echoes that orcas use to find prey?

6 What is the name for a killer whale family group?

7 At what age do female killer whales typically start breeding?

8 If a killer whale's dorsal fin is bent over, what can it mean?

9 What is the name of the famous killer whale featured in *Blackfish*?

10 What age can a female orca live to in the wild?

Killer whale quiz answers

1 Saddle patch
(page 7)

2 Its blowhole
(page 8)

3 50 kilometres per hour
(31 miles per hour)
(page 11)

4 250 kilograms
(551 pounds)
(page 13)

5 Echolocation
(page 14)

6 A pod
(page 17)

7 15
(page 19)

8 That the killer whale is
stressed and unhappy
(page 21)

9 Tilikum
(page 22)

10 80 to 90
(page 19)

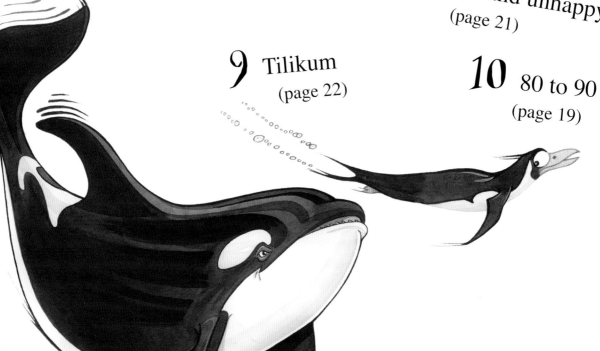

Killer whale facts

The largest orca ever recorded was 9.8 metres (32 feet) long.

The IUCN (International Union for Conservation of Nature) is unable to determine the species' conservation status, because global numbers of killer whales are unknown.

Killer whales can dive from 30 to 152 metres (100 to 500 feet) several times every day.

Killer whales swim up to 161 kilometres (100 miles) a day to exercise and hunt for food.

In 2005, the WWF (World Wide Fund for Nature) named killer whales the most toxic mammals in the Arctic. This meant that killer whales were found to contain higher levels of man-made toxic chemicals, including pesticides and pollutants, than any other species.

Where do toothed whales live?

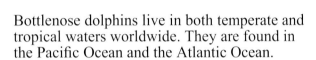

Whale and dolphin species inhabit all of the world's many oceans. The map below describes where killer whales and other related species live in the wild.

Bottlenose dolphins live in both temperate and tropical waters worldwide. They are found in the Pacific Ocean and the Atlantic Ocean.

Orca pods live in a very wide range of ocean habitats, from the warm waters around South Africa to the cold seas in the polar regions.

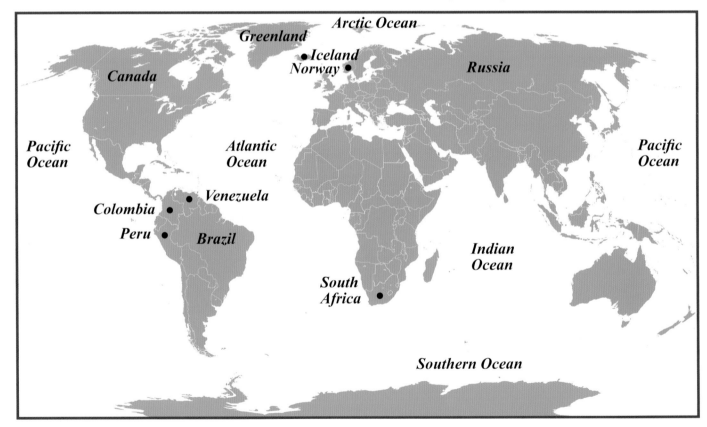

Amazon river dolphins are a freshwater dolphin that lives in the Amazon and Orinoco river basins in Brazil, Colombia, Peru, Venezuela and other South American countries.

Sperm whales can be found in every ocean in the world, but they avoid the very cold waters in the polar regions.

Glossary

Animal sanctuaries A type of nature reserve where animals are protected from harm.

Breach To break through something, such as water.

Calf The name for an infant whale or dolphin.

Dialect A specific form of a language used by a particular social group.

Habitat The natural environment of a particular animal or plant species.

Iceland An island country in the North Atlantic Ocean.

Insulated When something is protected from the loss of heat.

Lungs The organs that allow animals to absorb oxygen into their blood.

Mammals Animals, like humans, that are warm-blooded, have hair or fur and usually give birth to live babies.

Matriarchal A form of social organisation where a female is in charge of the group.

Pesticide A substance used to destroy insects and other organisms harmful to cultivated plants.

Predator An animal that eats other animals for food.

Streamlined When something has a shape that offers very little resistance to the flow of air or water, allowing increased speed of movement.

Toxin A type of poison, usually of plant or animal origin.

Index